The Poo Poo Book

A Book for Children to Enjoy and Learn about Toilet Time—Make Potty Training Easy and Fun!

A story by Mark and Mae Bacera

Illustrated by Kait Christenson and Mark Bacera

Disclaimers

(all the tough stuff and 'nutty' gritty)

Dedication and Thank You's

To Mae: May you grow up without boundaries and always remember that you are unique. Stay creative—never flush a good idea out of your mind.

To our friends and family: Thank you for helping out in so many ways. We love you!

To Kait, Debbie, Wendy, and the rest of the book team: We couldn't have done this without you. Thank you.

PART 1:
The Party Poopers

Peggy has an all-you-can-eat costume party

There are plates and plates of food, and many people as well.

GUEST LIST

Name	Costume
Prim	Popstar
Peter	Pirate
Paige	Policeofficer
Paul	Postman
Pepper	Princess
Patrick	Prince

But, in the end, Peggy and her pals eat too much...

Uh-oh...
Popstar Prim has a puffy tummy!

It's **potty** time!

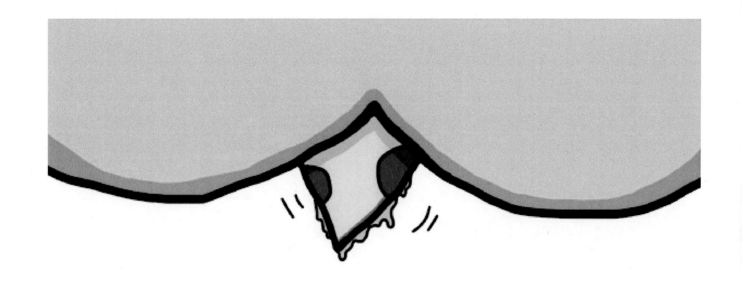

Something's coming out!

What is it!?

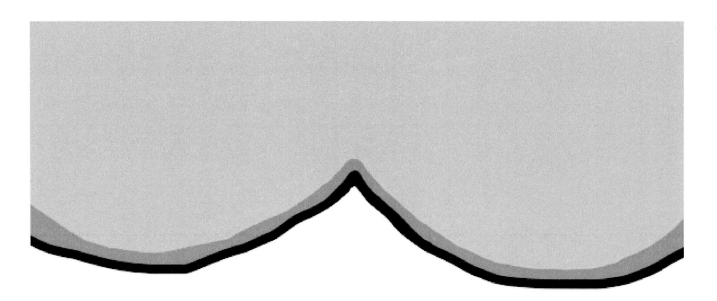

It's **PIZZA** !

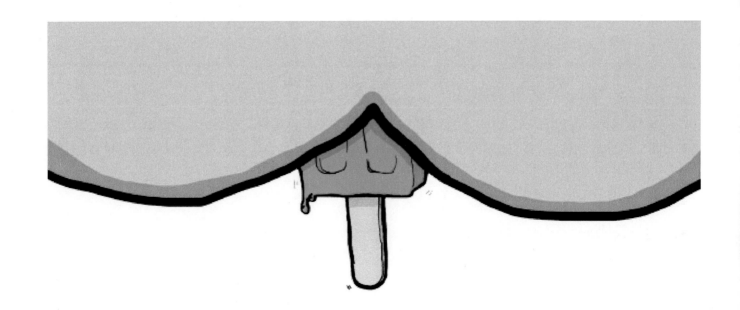

Something's coming out!

What is it!?

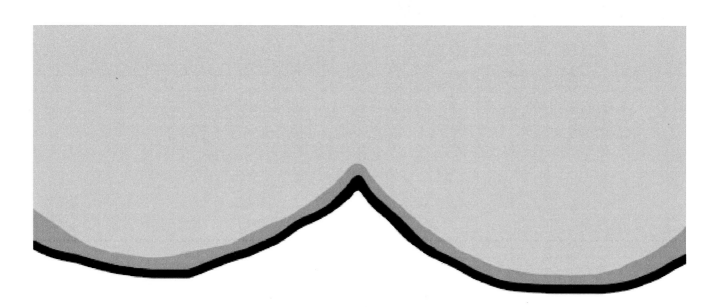

It's a **POPSICLE** !

Popstar Prim is pretty pleased!

Uh-oh...

Pirate Peter has a puffy tummy!

It's **potty** time!

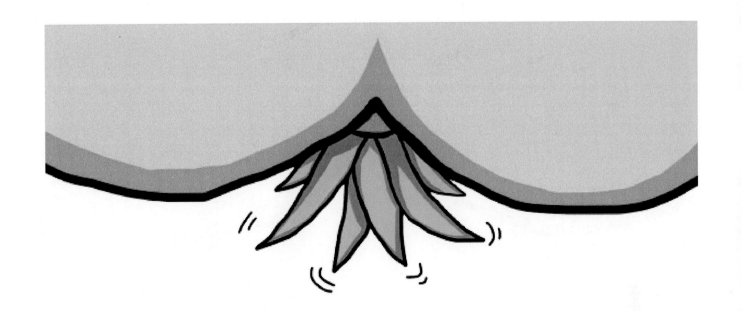

Something's coming out!

What is it!?

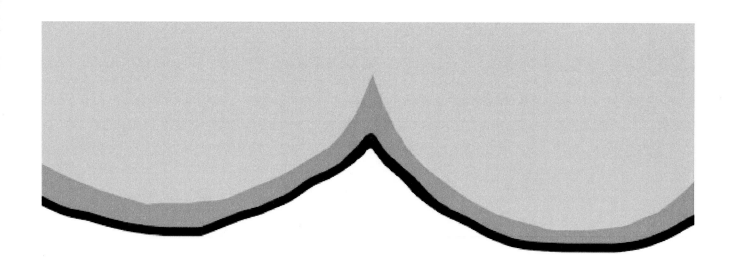

It's a **PINEAPPLE** !

Something's coming out!

What is it!?

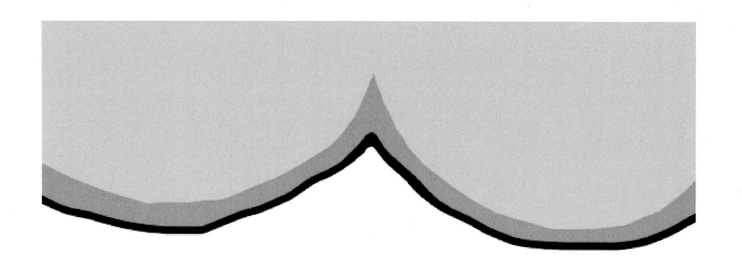

It's **POPCORN** !

Pirate Peter is pretty pleased!

Uh-oh...

Police Officer Paige

has a **puffy** tummy!

It's **potty** time!

Something's coming out!

What is it!?

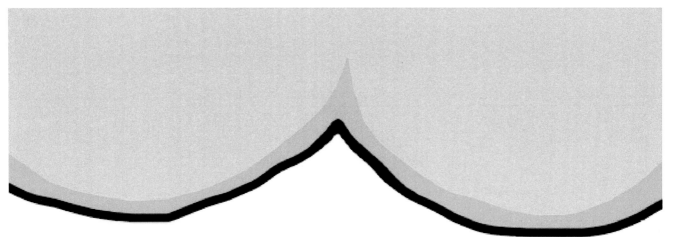

It's a **PEAR** !

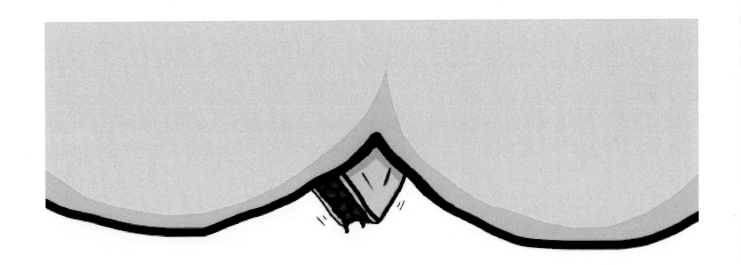

Something's coming out!

What is it!?

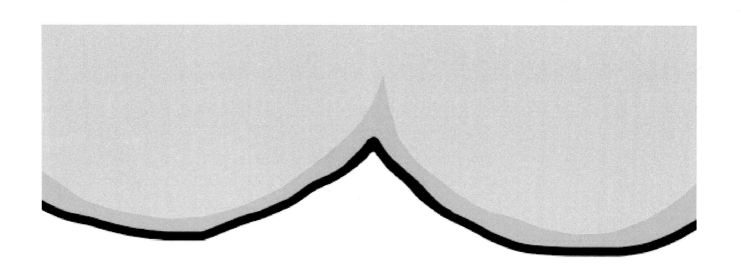

It's **PIE** !

Police officer Paige is pretty pleased!

Uh-oh...
Postman Paul has a puffy tummy!

It's **potty** time!

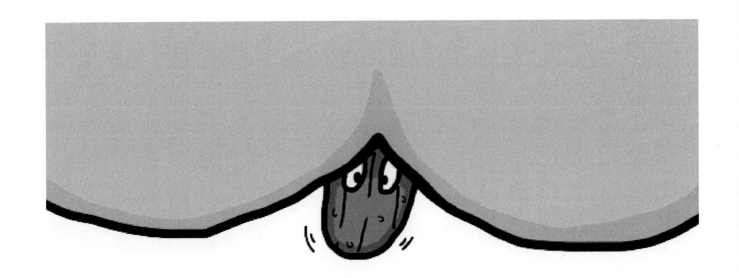

Something's coming out!

What is it!?

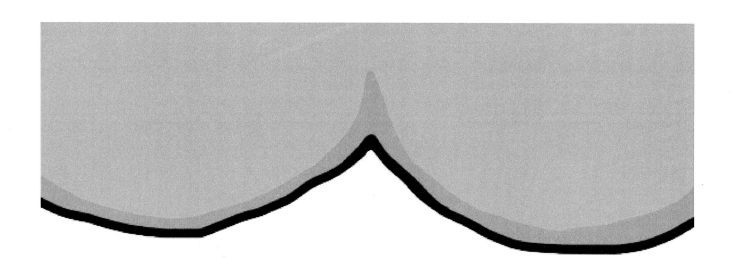

It's a **PICKLE** !

Something's coming out!

What is it!?

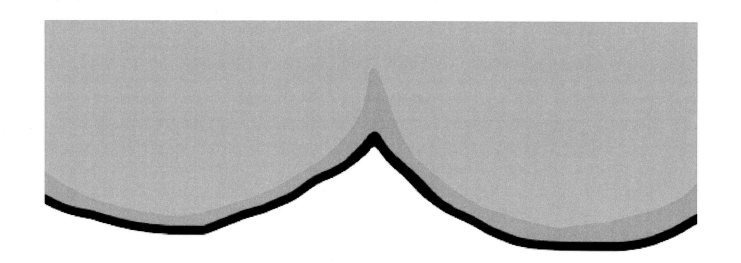

It's a **PEACH** !

Postman Paul is pretty pleased !

Knock knock.

Who's there?

I got up.

I got up, who?

I gotta poo! Open the door!

Uh-oh...

Princess Pepper has a puffy tummy!

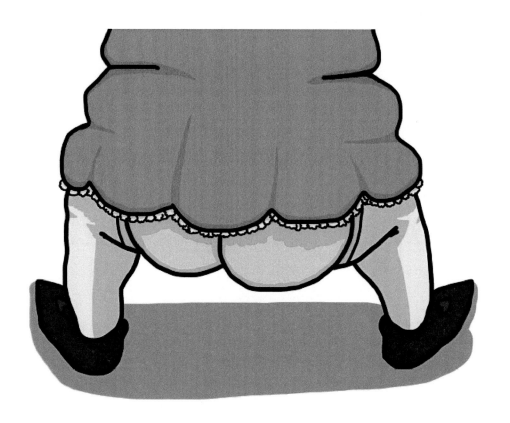

It's **potty** time!

Something's coming out!

What is it!?

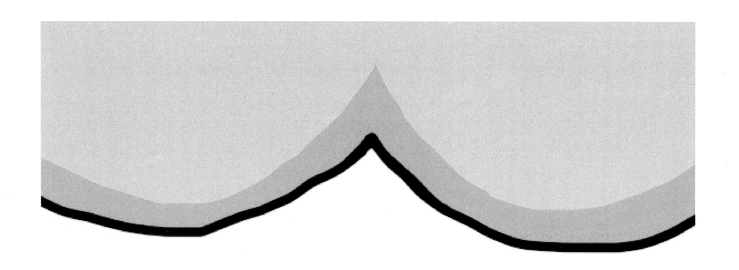

It's **PUDDING** !

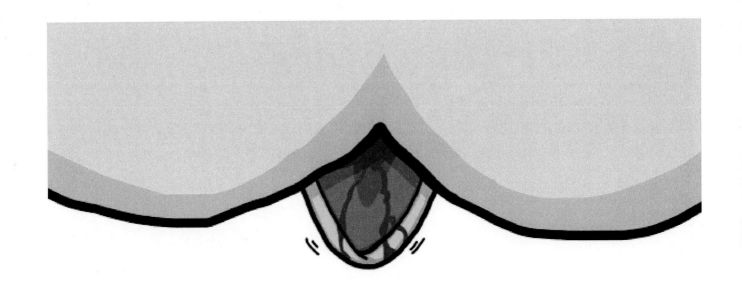

Something's coming out!

What is it!?

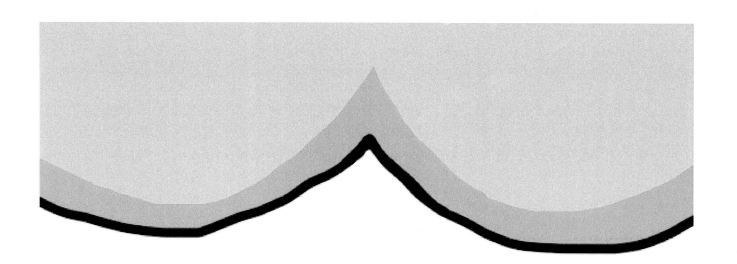

It's a **PANCAKE** !

Princess Pepper is pretty pleased!

My love for you is like poop...
...I can't hold it in...

Uh-oh...
Prince Patrick has a puffy tummy!

It's **potty** time!

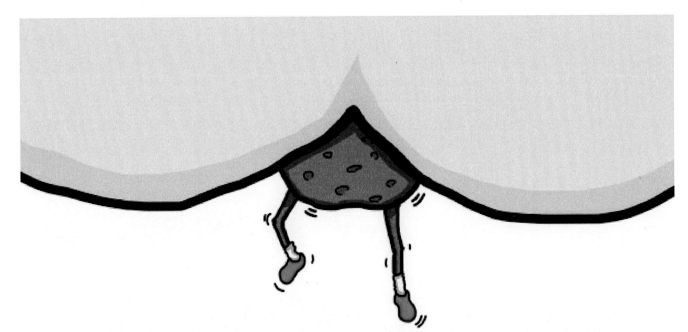

Something's coming out!

What is it!?

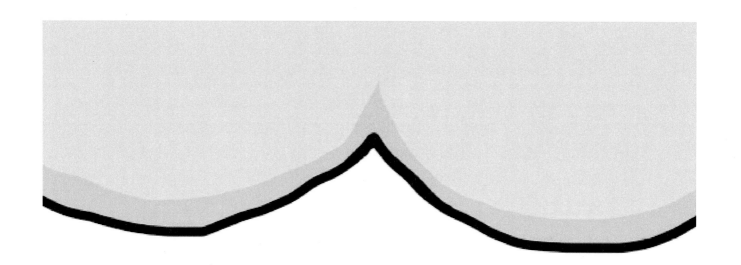

It's a **POTATO** !

Something's coming out!

What is it!?

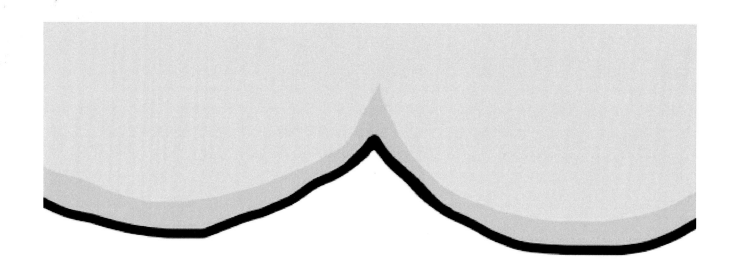

It's a **PRETZEL** !

Prince Patrick is pretty pleased!

What's long, brown, and sticky?

A STICK!

Uh-oh...

Preschooler Peggy

has a **puffy** tummy!

She **pulls** down
her **pants**!

She **pulls** down her **panties**!

Peggy sits on the potty!

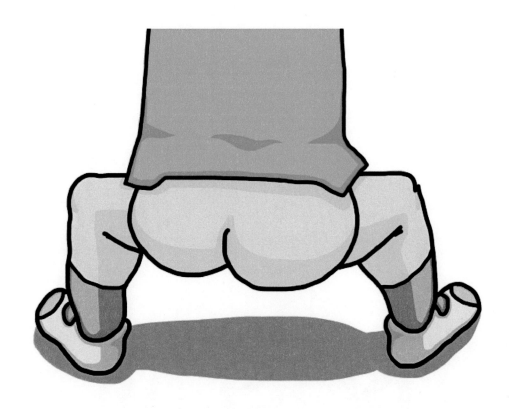

It's **potty** time!

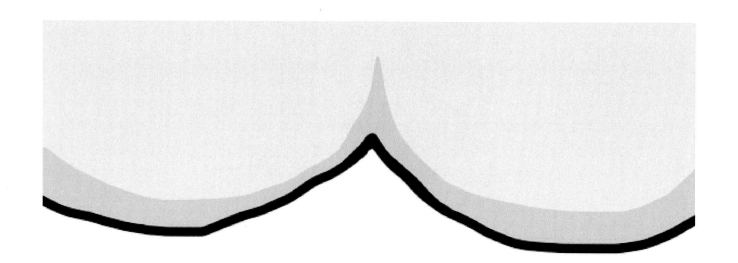

PUSH!!!

Something's coming out!

What is it!?

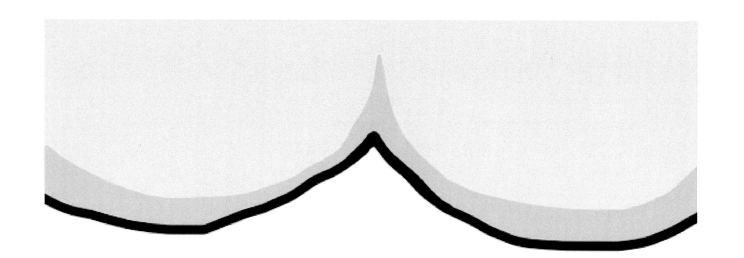

It's **Mr. Poo Poo** !

Toilet **paper** !

Done!

Time to flush!

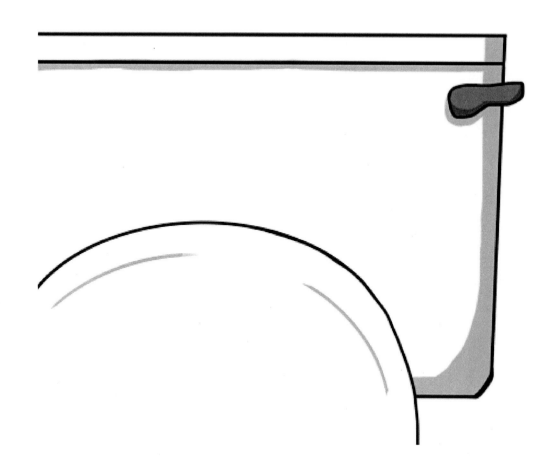

Bye bye!

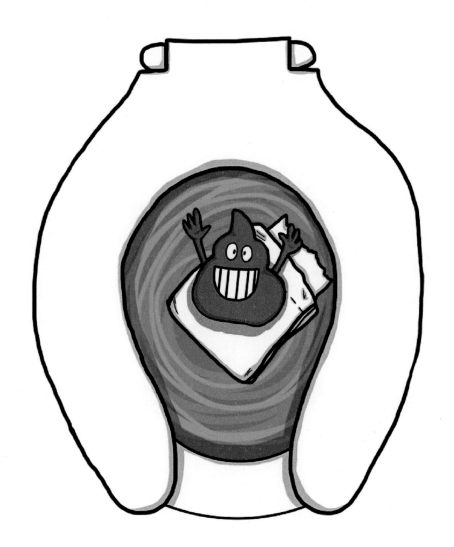

Peggy pulls up her **panties...**

pulls up her **pants...**

and washes her hands.

Preschooler Peggy is pretty pleased!

Perfect poopy potty time!

END (OF PART 1)

PART 2

Professor Poop's Presentation on Poop

Room 101

Hi, I'm Professor Poop.
I'll teach you about
good poop and bad poop.

First,
what shape is your poop?

SAUSAGE OR ICE CREAM SHAPE

SMOOTH

SOFT

 This is the best kind of poop. Positively perfect!

SEPARATE CLUMPS

HARD

If you see this, it means you don't eat enough fiber or drink enough liquids. So, drink more water and snack on more fruits & veggies!

This is like the last one, but bigger! Eat even more fruits & veggies. And drink an extra 2 to 4 glasses of water a day!

This can be normal, but it still means you have to drink more water.

Not bad! This is normal if you poop 2 or 3 times a day!

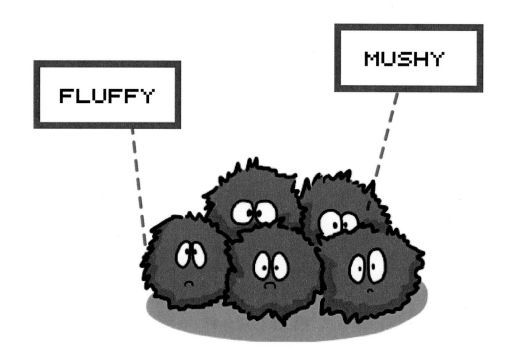

Still okay, but could mean something bad in your body. If this continues for multiple days, please tell a parent!

You have diarrhea. You probably have a virus or infection and this is how your body cleans it out. Tell a parent and drink lots of liquids!

This may mean that you've been eating too many oily foods. Cut back on the grease and see what happens! If it continues, tell a parent.

Okay, that's it for shape.
Now, let's talk about color.

What color is your poop?

Brown: This is perfect! Poop is naturally brown due to  natural fluids made in your body.

Green: This is also okay. Usually this color is due to eating a lot of green leafy veggies, or even green food coloring!

Yellow: This color of poop is often accompanied by a rancid or greasy smell. You could be  eating too much fatty foods!

Black: Danger! This could mean that you're bleeding internally! But, this color could also be made by having too much  of certain vitamins. If it's sticky tell a parent!

Red: Danger! This is usually caused by blood in your poop. Always tell a parent!

White: Or light-colored, or clay-colored poop is not normal. It can be caused by some medicines, or by a problem in  your body. Tell a parent!

And that's it! Just remember, if your poop looks different: TELL A PARENT!

END (OF PART 2)

Thank you for reading!

THE END

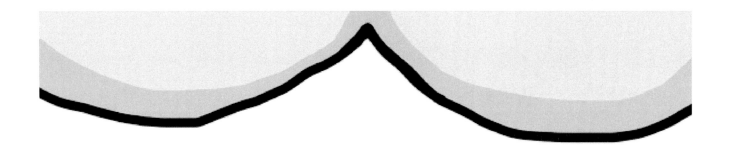

About the ~~Authors~~ Creators

Hi, I'm Mark and Mae is my daughter (she was four when we started this book). One day Mae had a terribly high fever so we rushed her to the doctor's clinic. Like any preschooler, Mae hates nurses and doctors. As soon as the nurse finished her preliminary questions and checkup, it was all we could do to stop Mae from crying like a baby (a two-year-old one). We rummaged through a box of toys and tried every one of them to no avail.

It was then that we found an old Etch A Sketch®. Things were so innocent at first; we drew hearts, cats, dogs, and every other cute thing on planet Earth. After exhausting all my cute ideas, for some strange reason, I drew a big round W and thought to myself that it looked very much like a butt.

And that's when 'poop' started to happen.

Random things started coming out of the butt, from hamburgers to elephants and to airplanes, you name it. In the end, it did its job; Mae smiled and laughed and was even able to endure the rest of her doctor's visit. Success.

We decided afterwards to try to make a book out of this concept and other various points: I picked the P theme, grabbed a list of p-names, p-jobs, and p-foods from the internet, and Mae decided on the combination of names, jobs, and foods.

We hope you liked it and hope you'll support us in our next project!

Mark and Mae Bacera

Amazon Author Page: https://www.amazon.com/Mark-Bacera/e/B0198EHT0M
Facebook: https://www.facebook.com/gokub
Email: markbacera@yahoo.com

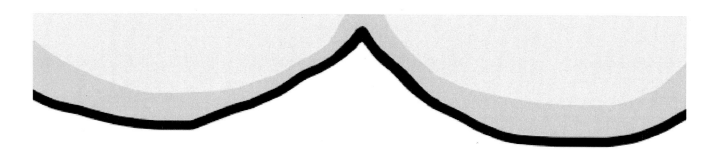

Other Books and Creations

- The Belly Button Book
- The Fart Book
- The Booger Book
- The Stinky Feet Book
- The Ear Wax Book
- The Sweat Book
- The Tear Book
- The Spit Book

Please note that some of the above titles have not yet been published.
To support us and be notified when new books are in the works and released,
send us an email at markbacera@yahoo.com